BUG BOOKS

Grasshopper

Karen Hartley, Chris Macro, and Philip Taylor

Heinemann Library
Chicago, Illinois

Customer Service 888-454-2279
Visit our website at www.heinemannraintree.com

Designed by Ron Kamen, Michelle Lisseter, and Bridge Creative Services Limited
Illustrations by Alan Fraser at Pennant Illustration
Printed in China by South China Printing Company

14 13 12 11
10 9 8 7 6 5 4

New edition ISBN: 1-4034-8297-7 (hardcover)   978-1-4034-8297-6 (hardcover)
                 1-4034-8310-8 (paperback)   978-1-4034-8310-2 (paperback)

The Library of Congress has cataloged the first edition as follows:
Hartley, Karen, 1949-
        Grasshopper / Karen Hartley, Chris Macro, and Philip Taylor.
            p. cm. -- (Bug books)
        Includes bibliographical references and index.
        Summary: A simple introduction to the physical characteristics, diet, life cycle, predators,
                habitat, and lifespan of grasshoppers.
        ISBN 1-57572-798-6 (lib. bdg.)
        1. Grasshoppers—Juvenile literature. [1. Grasshoppers.] I. Macro, Chris, 1940-. II. Taylor,
        Philip, 1949-. III. Title. IV. Series.
        QL508.A2H325   1999
        595.7'26—dc21   98-42674
                               CIP
                               AC

Acknowledgments
The author and publishers are grateful to the following for permission to reproduce photographs:
Ardea: p. 8, J Daniels p. 17, P Goetgheluck pp. 5, 11, 13, 14, 24, J Mason p. 10; Bruce Coleman
Limited: J Burton p. 25, W Cheng Ward p. 12, M Fogden p. 7, H Reinhard p. 20, K Taylor pp. 6,
26; Corbis: N J Dennis p. 21; Garden and Wildlife Matters: p. 27; Getty Images/The Image Bank:
M Mead p. 16; Trevor Clifford: pp. 28, 29; NHPA: S Dalton pp. 18, 21, 22, H and V Ingen p. 15;
Okapia: P Clay p. 23, M Wendler p. 4; Oxford Scientific Films: L Crowhurst p. 9.

Cover photograph reproduced with permission of Getty Images/The Image Bank.

The publishers would like to thank Nancy Harris for her assistance in the preparation of this book.

Some words are shown in bold, **like this**. You can find out what they mean
by looking in the glossary.

Contents

What Are Grasshoppers?

Grasshoppers are **insects**. They have six legs. There are many different types of grasshoppers.

Some grasshoppers are called **crickets**. Some large grasshoppers are called **locusts**.

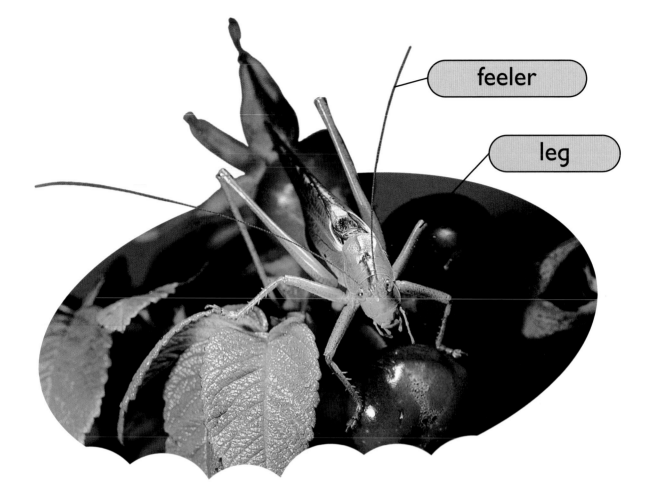

feeler

leg

Grasshoppers have long bodies. They
have four long wings and large eyes.
They have two **feelers** on their heads.
The two back legs of a grasshopper
are much longer than the other four.

Grasshoppers have very hard skin
that is green or brown. This one
is the same color as the plants it
lives on.

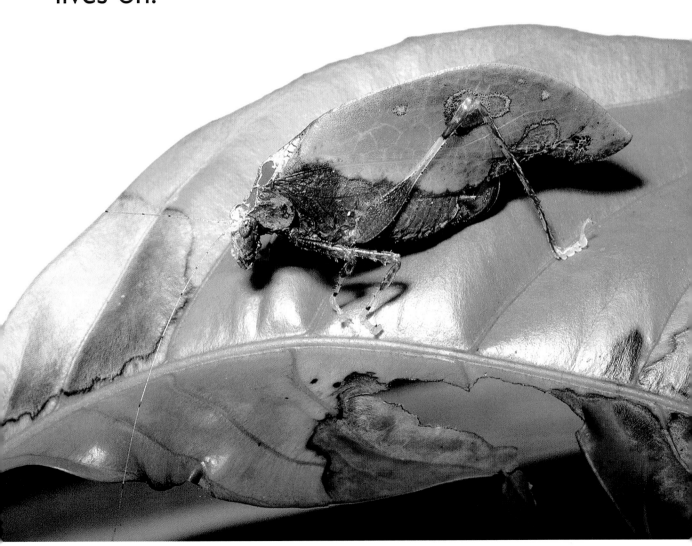

Some grasshoppers are much bigger than others. Many grasshoppers are about as long as your little finger.

8

female

male

Female grasshoppers are a bit longer than the **males**. Apart from the difference in size, the males and females look alike.

9

How Are Grasshoppers Born?

The **female** grasshopper lays about 100 eggs in late summer. She covers them with a sticky liquid. This gets hard and protects them.

Young grasshoppers **hatch** out of the eggs in spring. They are very small. They look like **adults** without normal wings.

How Do Grasshoppers Grow?

Grasshoppers grow very quickly.
When they get too big, their skin splits.
The grasshopper crawls out. A new skin
has grown underneath the old one.
This is called **molting**.

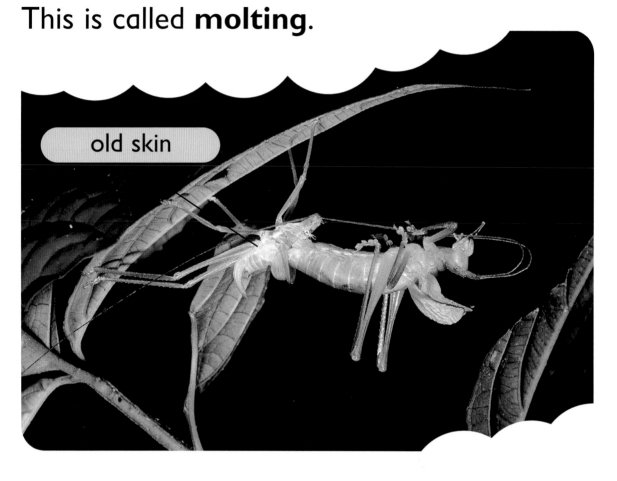

old skin

Grasshoppers molt four to six times before they are grown up. When they are bigger the new skins have wings.

What Do Grasshoppers Eat?

Grasshoppers have strong jaws called **mandibles**. They use them to cut and chew the grass and leaves that they eat. Some **crickets** eat caterpillars, snails, and worms.

mandibles

Locusts are large grasshoppers. They live in big groups called **swarms**. They can eat fields of crops in a short time.

Which Animals Eat Grasshoppers?

Most grasshoppers are attacked when they are still in the egg, or when they are very young. Spiders eat them if they land on their webs. Birds, snakes, and lizards also eat grasshoppers.

Frogs and newts catch grasshoppers
with their long tongues.

How Do Grasshoppers Move?

Grasshoppers usually move by jumping. They have very long back legs to give a strong push off the ground. They can jump very high.

All grasshoppers have large wings,
but only **locusts** are good at flying.

Where Do Grasshoppers Live?

Grasshoppers live in nearly every country. Most grasshoppers live in thick grassy areas or in the woods.

Some grasshoppers live in houses and some live under the ground. Others live in sand dunes and some live on cliffs.

How Long Do Grasshoppers Live?

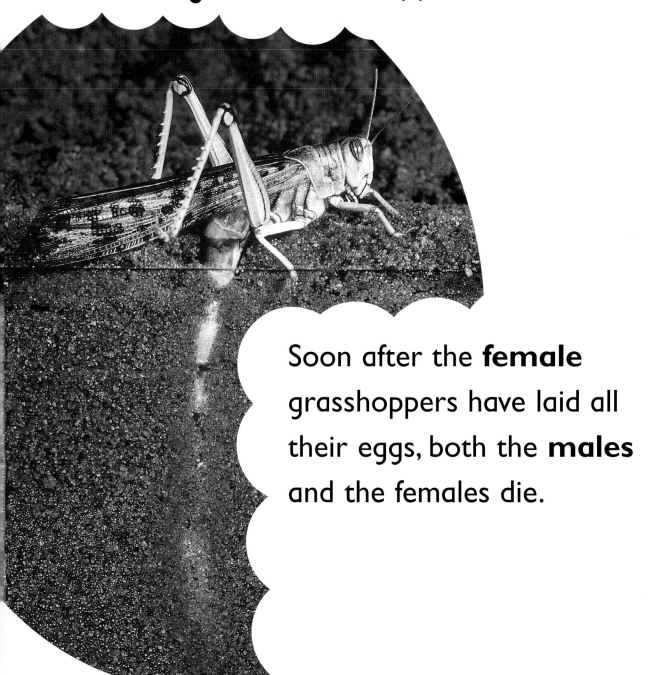

Soon after the **female** grasshoppers have laid all their eggs, both the **males** and the females die.

Grasshoppers cannot live through
a cold winter, but the eggs survive.
They **hatch** in the spring.

eggs

How Are Grasshoppers Special?

Male grasshoppers can make a singing noise. They rub the bumps on their back legs along the hard edges of their wings to make the noise.

Male grasshoppers sing to attract **females**.

Male grasshoppers spend a lot of time on grass stalks. Their singing can last all day and all night.

Each type of grasshopper has a different song. The **females** know which is the right song for them.

Thinking About Grasshoppers

These two children are looking for grasshoppers. They can hear them in the grass. They want to watch what the grasshoppers do for a day or two.

They have brought a plastic cage with
them. What will they need to put into
the cage so the grasshoppers can live
there? Where would be the best place
to put the cage?

Bug Map

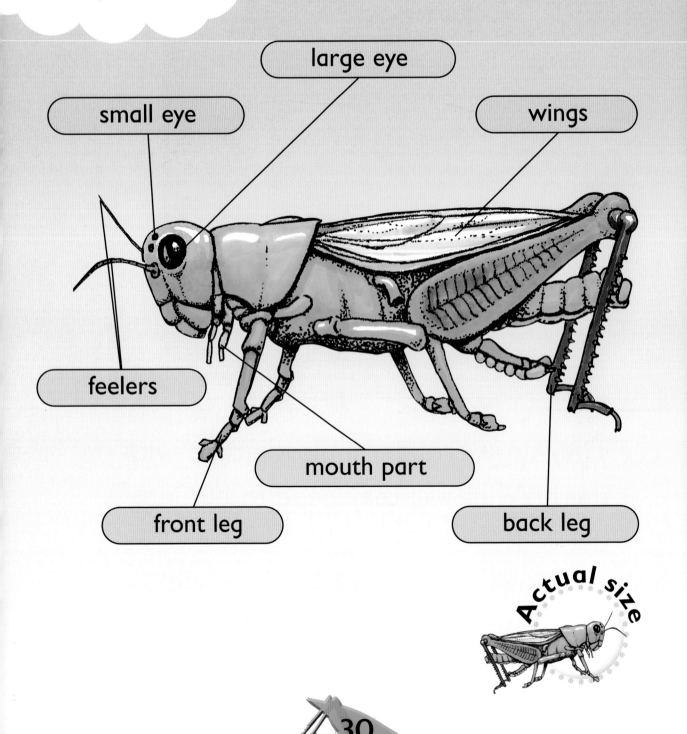

large eye

small eye

wings

feelers

mouth part

front leg

back leg

Actual size

Glossary

adult grown-up

cricket type of grasshopper with very long feelers

feelers thin growths from the head of an insect that help the insect know what is around it

female girl

hatch to come out of an egg

insect small animal with six legs

locust type of large grasshopper that usually lives in hot countries

male boy

mandibles parts of the mouths of insects, used for biting and chewing

molting when a grasshopper grows too big for its skin, it grows a new one. The old one falls off.

swarm a large group of many, many insects

Index

More Books to Read

Pyers, Greg. *Grasshoppers Up Close.*
　Chicago: Raintree, 2005.